MW00452433

IMAGES
of America
MARYLAND'S
MOTION PICTURE
THEATERS

ON THE COVER: The Broadway Theater (509 South Broadway, Baltimore) was built in 1916 to replace an earlier Broadway that had burned the previous year. The second Broadway lasted until 1977. The building is still standing; it has been used as a club and restaurant since it closed. (Photograph courtesy of the author.)

IMAGES
of America

MARYLAND'S
MOTION PICTURE
THEATERS

Robert K. Headley

ARCADIA
PUBLISHING

Copyright © 2008 by Robert K. Headley
ISBN 978-0-7385-5384-9

Published by Arcadia Publishing
Charleston SC, Chicago IL, Portsmouth NH, San Francisco CA

Printed in the United States of America

Library of Congress Catalog Card Number: 2007942637

For all general information contact Arcadia Publishing at:
Telephone 843-853-2070
Fax 843-853-0044
E-mail sales@arcadiapublishing.com
For customer service and orders:
Toll-Free 1-888-313-2665

Visit us on the Internet at www.arcadiapublishing.com

To Anne, for everything.

CONTENTS

ACKNOWLEDGMENTS

It took a lot of help to put this book together. I would like to thank the following people and organizations for making this possible: Herbert Harwood Jr., Sue Fischer (U.S. Naval Training Center Bainbridge Association), Historical Society of Howard County, Cassandra Pritts (Brooke Whiting Archives), Danyelle R. Dorsey (Baltimore Museum of Industry), Paul Berry (Calvert Marine Museum), Laura Linke (Carl A. Kroch Library, Cornell University), Mike Miklas (Bainbridge USNTC Historical Society), Paul Sanchez, Roger Russell, Gary Helton, Robert W. Barnes, Karen Sykes (Calvert County Historical Society), Mike Dixon (Cecil County Historical Society), Francis "Sonny" Callahan, Jeanne Townsend (Worcester County Library), Helen Heath (Garrett County Historical Society), Don Gunther, William Hollifield, Pat Taylor (Edward H. Nabb Research Center for Delmarva History and Culture), C. H. Echols and the Dundalk and Patapsco Neck Historical Society, Ed Dobbins, Roger White, Mark Schatz (Anne Arundel County Historical Society), Jennie Levine (Hornbake Library, University of Maryland, College Park), Marsha Wise, Barbara Taylor (Fort George G. Meade Museum), Faye Haskins (D.C. Public Library), the Honorable Lawrence H. Rushworth, and Tom Kiefaber (Senator Theater). I apologize if I have missed anyone. Unless otherwise noted, the images are from my collection.

I hope you will find pictures of theaters here that bring back happy memories. If you find any errors or if you have any additions, please let me know. Now step back into time. Let's go to the movies!

Robert K. Headley
University Park, MD
August 2007

INTRODUCTION

Sadly, most of the movie theaters that have been built in the state of Maryland are gone. Many have disappeared without leaving any traces except fading advertisements in microfilmed newspapers. Some have been demolished. Others have been remodeled and are scarcely recognizable. A few are still in business.

They were babysitters and schools. They were the places for first dates and to hide from the horrors of world wars and laugh at Abbott and Costello. Dark and cool in the summer, warm and cozy in the winter, they were places used to escape from reality for a few hours. Some were palaces where one could experience grandeur that would impress royalty; others were rough-hewn buildings of a more modest style. They were called movie theaters or movie houses or nickelodeons or, to the more sophisticated late-20th-century audiences, cinemas, multiplexes, and megaplexes. In Baltimore, they were simply called "movies," and listeners figured out whether that meant the place or the film. This book is a tribute to them all, new ones as well as older theaters, fossilized theaters, and working theaters. No attempt is made here to catalog all of the movie theaters that have ever existed in the state and district. It has been necessary to pick and choose, selecting interesting, attractive, famous, or unique theaters.

At one time, there were more than 200 movie theaters in Maryland. The destruction of these theaters has been horrifying. The figures for Baltimore are striking. Out of 89 movie theaters operating there in 1955, only two are still operating as movie theaters. All of the downtown theaters in Annapolis are out of business, as are the ones in Dundalk, Havre de Grace, Ellicott City, Elkton, Bel Air, Denton, Federalsburg, Cambridge, Salisbury, Lonaconing, Oakland, and Crisfield. Among the most egregious losses are those of the Maryland and Strand in Cumberland, the Druid in Damascus, the Circle in Annapolis, the Flower in Silver Spring, the Belair in Bel Air, the Boulevard in Salisbury, the Pikes in Pikesville, the Cinema I and II in Lutherville, the Elk in Elkton, and Ford's, the Ambassador, Stanley, Century, Grand, Auditorium-Mayfair, Parkway, and Gayety in Baltimore.

But not all has been lost. Bright lights in Maryland's theater scene are the Weinburg Center (former Tivoli) in Frederick, the Carroll in Westminster, the Maryland in Hagerstown, the Embassy in Cumberland, the Palace in Frostburg, the Avalon in Easton, the Lyceum in Chestertown, the Churchill in Church Hill, the Public Playhouse in Cheverly, the Greenbelt in Greenbelt, the Mar-Va in Pocomoke City, and the Senator and Hippodrome in Baltimore.

Movies arrived in Maryland in 1894 when visitors to the Columbia Phonograph's store in downtown Baltimore could see movies on Thomas Edison's kinetoscope. Soon entrepreneurs realized that a roomful of people could watch a movie if it could be projected on a screen or wall. Projected movies came to Maryland in 1896, and movie shows began to appear throughout the state. Some of these were in Baltimore at Electric Park in 1896, in Annapolis at the Opera House in 1901, in Cumberland at the Academy of Music in 1898, in Preston at the Methodist church in 1900, and in Frederick at the City Opera House in 1898.

Around 1906, people began to think about places filled with seats where movies could be shown on a permanent basis. Budding exhibitors took existing stores, gutted them, decorated the fronts, and installed seats. They added screens, sat a piano player under the screen, and built tiny booths for the primitive projectors. With a staff made up of friends and family as cashiers, doormen, ushers, and projectionists, they were ready to make their fortunes. Of the hundreds of early exhibitors who opened movie theaters in the first two decades of the 20th century, only a few lasted into the 1920s. Running a successful movie theater depended on many things; location was a major consideration.

The decade between 1920 and 1930 saw the biggest movie theaters ever built in the state. They were not only huge, but they were also opulent and luxurious. They could seat the population of a small town. Just about every city with a population of more than 10,000 people had one of these palaces. Baltimore had many—the Stanley and Century were the biggest—but there were also the State, New, Rivoli, Boulevard, Capitol, Belnord, and McHenry. Frederick and Hagerstown each had one, and Cumberland had several. There were other movie palaces scattered around the state; the Avalon in Easton and the Circle in Annapolis come to mind.

Many neighborhoods and towns in Maryland got their first real movie theaters in the 1930s and 1940s. Modern movie houses were opened in Federalsburg, Waldorf, La Plata, Damascus, Upper Marlboro, and Pikesville, and in Baltimore in Westport, Howard Park, Govanstown, and Forest Park. Drive-ins first appeared in the state in Glen Burnie in 1939. In the 1950s, just about all of the few new theaters that opened were drive-ins.

The 1960s saw the end of the single-screen theater. Coming after a bleak period of theater building when scarcely anything was built except drive-ins, four-wall theaters of the 1960s were magnificent. By today's standards they were huge; most seated around 1,000. These plain theaters featured large lobbies with glass fronts, wide screens, and big concessions counters. Few of these great single-screen theaters remain. The Holiday in Frederick and the Laurel Cinema are the only ones presently operating in the state, but both have been remodeled and subdivided into smaller auditoriums. The Riverdale Plaza Theater in Riverdale still stands in good condition, but it has been closed for many years. The Hillendale in Baltimore is now a church after several failed attempts to keep it going.

Multiple auditoriums became the hallmark of movie theaters after the mid-1960s, but the first multi-auditorium theater in the state was Lubin's theater in the old Colonnade building at 404 East Baltimore Street in Baltimore. Sigmund Lubin opened two theaters here in the spring of 1907. The downstairs theater showed movies while the theater on the second and third floors was devoted to vaudeville. Lubin also had a small theater next door for a couple of years. Could this have been the first triplex in the country? Then, in 1926, the Valencia Theater was built in the dance hall on top of Baltimore's Century Theater. But multi-auditorium theaters did not catch on, and it was many years before the next one was built in the state. In August 1964, Schwaber Theaters opened their Cinema I and II in the Yorkridge Shopping Center. Roth's Seven Locks twin opened in Rockville in 1968. After 1970, no more single auditorium theaters were built in the state. Twin theaters morphed into quads, and quads became 10-plexes. In 1995, R/C Theaters opened a 10-screen complex on Eastern Avenue opposite East Point Shopping Center in Baltimore County. This was the first megaplex in the state. Auditorium Four at East Point is one of the finest recent auditoriums. By 1998, megaplexes with 14 and 16 auditoriums seating more than 3,000 people were being built. At the end of the century, Florida-based Muvico opened the biggest of them all. Muvico's 24-screen megaplex at Arundel Mills, which can seat more than 5,000 people, brought back the glitz of the great movie palaces of the late 1920s. By 2007, there were 21 megaplexes operating in Maryland.

One

BALTIMORE CITY

The earliest recorded showing of movies in Maryland was on June 16, 1896, at Electric Park, a large, suburban amusement park on Belvedere Avenue in what is now Pimlico. The Vitascope exhibitions at Electric Park became popular, and soon there were other exhibitions of moving pictures in Baltimore. In 1906, the first movie theater in town opened in the 400 block of East Baltimore Street. After that, little movie theaters began opening all over town. Among the early ones were the Wizard Theaters on West Lexington and Eutaw Streets, the Ideal and Amusea on Eutaw Street, the Paradise on Fleet Street, the Cupid on Light Street, the Leader, Bijou-Dream, Nicoland, Family, and Arcadia on South Broadway, Fairyland on Chester Street, and the Bon-Ton, Daisy, and Graphic on North Gay Street. By 1910, there were about 98 movie theaters operating in Baltimore. Larger theaters were built after 1914 and especially in the 1920s when several 1,000-seat neighborhood theaters opened. Theaters spread out of the older neighborhoods into the suburbs during the 1930s and 1940s. Beginning in the 1950s, Baltimore began losing theaters, a trend that has sadly continued up to this day.

Certainly, no one can deny that the mighty Stanley Theater was the most magnificent movie theater in Baltimore. In spite of its ignominious end, torn down under another name for a parking lot, the Stanley is at the head of the list of superlatives among Maryland's movie houses. It was the largest and the most lavishly decorated. It had the most varieties of marble (five) and probably the longest throw from projection booth to screen in the state. By all rights, this wonderful building should still stand on North Howard Street. Other important theaters in Baltimore included the Hippodrome, the Century, the Little, which was the first art theater in the state, the Ambassador, Metropolitan, Ford's, Royal, Playhouse, and Senator.

The ancient Holliday Street Theater in the 100 block of North Holliday Street was an early venue for movies in Baltimore. The structure shown here is dated from 1874, but there had been a theater on the site since 1795. Films were shown here as early as 1898. It was torn down in 1918, one of the first in a long list of casualties in Baltimore's war against theaters.

Blaney's, named after New York theater man Charles E. Blaney, opened in February 1903. It was built in what had earlier been St. Mark's Church. This theater had many names over its lifetime: Empire, Oriole, Blaney's, Savoy, Colonial, and Playhouse. It closed in 1922. Hutzler's Department Store acquired the building in 1934 and used it as an annex until the 1980s. It was demolished in 1986.

The grand old legitimate theater of Baltimore, Ford's (320 West Fayette Street), opened in 1871 and closed after many remodelings in 1964. One of the most historic theaters in the state, it was destroyed to make space for a parking garage. (*News-American* photograph courtesy of Special Collections, University of Maryland Libraries.)

Early movies were shown in Ford's in 1896, and popular road show films, including *The Birth of a Nation*, were shown there until the late 1920s. The interior is similar to that of several of Thomas Lamb's designs, including the Maryland Theater in Hagerstown and the Tivoli in Washington, D.C. (Photograph courtesy of Special Collections, University of Maryland Libraries.)

The Academy of Music, Baltimore, Md.

One of at least four Academies of Music in the state, the Baltimore Academy (516 North Howard Street) was the largest and most elaborate. It could seat more than 3,000 people in several halls. It opened in January 1875 and lasted until 1926, when it was replaced by the Stanley Theater.

The Maryland Theater (320–322 West Franklin Street) opened in 1903 as part of James Kernan's Million Dollar Triple Enterprise. Although it was primarily a live theater, the Maryland did show movies. It showed some of the earliest films in Baltimore, including *The Great Baltimore Fire* and *The Great Train Robbery* in 1904. Famous actors, including Eva Tanguay, W. C. Fields, Jack Benny, Henry Fonda, Fanny Brice, and Houdini appeared at the Maryland. It closed and was demolished in 1951.

The history of the Monumental Theater (725 East Baltimore Street) started in 1837 when the Washington Hall Theater opened. The theater burned in 1874. It was rebuilt as the New Central Theater in 1875. Soon after it reopened, it was renamed the Monumental, which lasted until 1928, when it was destroyed by another fire. The Monumental, renamed the Folly in 1917, presented an eclectic assortment of shows from Yiddish theater to movies, burlesque, boxing matches, and wrestling. Local wrestling champ Gus Schoenlein, better known as "Americus," got his start at the Monumental in 1903. (*News-American* photograph courtesy of Special Collections, University of Maryland Libraries.)

The Lyceum (1209 North Charles Street) started out in 1879 as a respectable performing arts venue and ended up being denounced from the pulpit by a minister who said he was happy about the fire that destroyed it in 1925. Many well-known theatrical figures, including John W. Albaugh, Plimpton B. Chase, and George Fawcett, operated the Lyceum, and Sarah Bernhardt, Edwin Booth, and Helena Modjeska appeared on its stage. (*News-American* photograph courtesy of Special Collections, University of Maryland Libraries.)

The Lyric Theater (130 Mount Royal Avenue) is one of the great theaters in the state. Not noted for showing motion pictures, the Lyric was nevertheless one of the major venues for early films in Baltimore. It opened in 1895 as the Music Hall, but the name was changed to Lyric in 1903. The name "Music Hall" was thought to be lower class. The 2,000-seat Lyric boasts some of the finest acoustics in the country. (Postcard photograph courtesy of William Hollifield.)

Electric Park (Belvedere Avenue, West Arlington) was one of the amusement parks built around Baltimore to lure people to ride streetcars out to the cooler suburbs. It opened in June 1896 and was the site of the first projected movies in the state. Electric Park delighted thousands of Marylanders until it closed in 1915. All traces of the park have disappeared.

14

One of the most interesting theaters in the state, the Auditorium (508 North Howard Street) started life around 1866 as a music hall. In 1880, it became the Natatorium. James Kernan acquired it in 1890 and changed the name to the Howard Auditorium. After several remodelings, in 1903, the Auditorium became part of Kernan's Million Dollar Triple Enterprise, which also included the Maryland Theater and the Kernan Hotel. The Auditorium was a major venue for early movies, musicals, and vaudeville. In 1940, a movie theater, the Mayfair, was built within the shell of the Auditorium. The Mayfair operated until 1986. It has been closed since then. A roof collapse in 1998 has made restoring the old theater problematic. (Photograph courtesy of the Baltimore County Public Library Legacy Web.)

The Auditorium and Academy of Music are side by side in the 500 block of Baltimore's North Howard Street. Not too long after this photograph was taken, the Academy of Music was demolished to build the Stanley. (*News-American* photograph courtesy of Special Collections, University of Maryland Libraries.)

The Gayety Theater (405 East Baltimore Street) was the longtime home of burlesque in Baltimore. It was designed by the popular theater architect J. B. McElfatrick and opened in February 1906. (*News-American* photograph courtesy of Special Collections, University of Maryland Libraries.)

All of the well-known burlesque performers, including Gypsy Rose Lee, Blaze Starr, Ann Corio, Red Skelton, and Joe Penner, appeared on the Gayety's stage. In the winter of 1969, the Gayety was seriously damaged in a fire and never reopened. The building is still standing.

The 400 block of East Baltimore Street with eight early theaters was the first home to movie exhibitions in Baltimore. On the right in this c. 1911 photograph is the Grand, followed by the two Lubin theaters. (Photograph courtesy of the Library of Congress, Prints and Photographs Division, Wittemann Collection, LC-USZ62-137479.)

This photograph of the block, taken a few years later, shows the Grand and Lubin theaters on the right and the Gayety and Victoria on the left. (*News-American* photograph courtesy of Special Collections, University of Maryland Libraries.)

The Leader Theater (248 South Broadway) had a long history. It was built by Joseph Berman in 1909 and closed in 1959. The Leader used behind-the-screen talkers to provide sound before talking films. Under the management of Maurice Cohen, it was one of the first movie theaters in Baltimore to get air-conditioning. The building is still standing, but it has been extensively remodeled.

This unique photograph of the Fairyland Theater (624 North Chester Street) has quite a history. It was rescued from a trash bin by George R. Scherman (1906–1981) and was restored by Ed Dobbins of Baltimore in 2007. The Fairyland was a tiny, 250-seat, neighborhood theater that lasted from 1908 to around 1927. Later the building was used as a church.

The intersection of North Charles Street and North Avenue was the home of four theaters, a multi-purpose casino, a radio station, and a market. The Aurora (7 East North Avenue) and its neighbor, the Theatorium (11 East North Avenue), were located just east of Charles Street. The Aurora was built by Eugene Cook in 1910. It closed 74 years later after several name changes. When it became the 7 East in the summer of 1960, it reopened with a showing of *Psycho*. (Photograph courtesy of the Baltimore Museum of Industry.)

The Dixie Theater (312 West Baltimore Street) opened in 1909. It seated just under 200 people. In 1936, the name was changed to Europa. As the Europa, it was one of the early art theaters in Maryland. But Maryland was not ready for art films, and the Europa closed in 1937. A terrible accident occurred in 1926 when one of the large statues on the theater's facade fell and killed a small child. (*News-American* photograph courtesy of Special Collections, University of Maryland Libraries.)

The facade of the Elektra Theater (1039 North Gay Street) was spectacular even by nickelodeon standards. The Elektra was designed by Theodore Wells Pietsch, who also designed the Wilson and Excelsior theaters. It opened in 1910 and closed in 1924. The building has been demolished.

This building has a long history, and it is not over yet. The Empire Theater (311 West Fayette Street) opened in 1911. It was designed by William H. McElfatrick and Otto Simonson. It got a new name in 1913: the Palace. Vaudeville and burlesque, along with movies, were the fare at the Palace. Faced with dwindling audiences, the Palace closed in 1936. It was converted into a garage the following year. In 1945, Isador Rappaport hired architects John Zink and Lucius R. White Jr. to turn it back into a movie theater. The Town Theater opened on January 22, 1947, with *It's a Wonderful Life*. The Town closed in 1990. In 2007, Everyman Theater announced that it would take over the building and use it for live performances.

Theodore Wells Pietsch designed the Excelsior (1358 West North Avenue) for the Benesch brothers in 1911. Pietsch's exuberant facades can also be seen in the Wilson and Elektra theaters. The extravagant facade was a mixed blessing; the theater was closed down late in its life because of the danger of falling plaster ornamentation. The Excelsior closed around 1926. (*News-American* photograph courtesy of Special Collections, University of Maryland Libraries.)

The Astor Theater (611 Poplar Grove Street) opened as the Popular Theater in 1913 (see page 123). It was one of many early Baltimore theaters designed by Frederick E. Beall. The name was changed to Astor when Robert Kanter remodeled the theater in 1927. The Astor closed in 1955 after a short stint as an African American theater. The building, which is still standing, was later used as a supermarket.

The Preston Theater (1108 East Preston Street) opened as the Flaming Arrow in the summer of 1913; it closed in 1944. It was designed for the Crescent Novelty Company by Frederick E. Beall, who designed 11 small theaters in Baltimore. See page 119 for a recent view of the Preston.

The Grand Theater (511 South Conkling Street) was Highlandtown's main movie theater. It was also one of the largest in southeast Baltimore. It opened in 1913 and closed in 1985. It could have made a rich contribution to the entertainment life of the city and the neighborhood, but it was demolished in 2000.

The tiny Govans Theater (5005 York Road) lasted only about seven years (1914–1921). It was immortalized in this photograph by the Roland Park Company, which wanted to show the dangers of allowing such disreputable buildings as movie theaters to be built in a community. (Roland Park Company Records, #2828 photograph courtesy of the Division of Rare and Manuscript Collections, Cornell University Library.)

THE HIPPODROME, EUTAW ST., BALTIMORE, MD.

It went from being a white elephant to one of Baltimore's most successful theaters. When it was built, people said that the Hippodrome (12 North Eutaw Street) was too far west of downtown. Owners Marion Pearce and Philip Scheck had Thomas W. Lamb design the Hippodrome; they opened it in November 1914 with vaudeville and movies. It was not successful until Isador Rappaport took it over in 1931; under Rappaport, it became one of the most popular theaters in town.

Most of the big-time film and vaudeville stars appeared on the Hippodrome's stage. Many remember seeing *The Tingler* and experiencing the thrill of the vibrating seats in the summer of 1959. The Hippodrome closed in 1990. After several years of uncertainty, the theater was restored with an expanded stage. It reopened in February 2004 and has become a major venue for Broadway shows.

The Fulton, which opened in 1915 as the Gertrude McCoy, became an African American theater in 1945. It lasted until 1952 when it was converted into a food market. It later became a church and was seriously damaged in a fire in 2007. This photograph, from about 1946, shows members of the Colored Operators' Protective Association attending a banquet at the Fulton.

The naming of movie theaters in the first half of the 20th century was quite different than it is today. Instead of "Cinema 1 and 2" or "Cinema 14," there were "Blue Mouse," "Wizard," "Excelsior," "Idle Hour," lots of "Gems" and "Palaces," and theaters named after people. The Gertrude McCoy Theater on Fulton Avenue in Baltimore was named after this silent film star who was a favorite of the exhibitor. Gertrude McCoy was born in 1890. She appeared in more than 100 films between 1911 and 1926. She died in Atlanta in 1967.

Several people have made valiant attempts to save the Parkway Theater (5 West North Avenue), but so far no one has succeeded. If there were ever a theater in need of saving, it is this one. Designed by Oliver Wight for Henry Webb in 1915, the Parkway is a jewel. Many of the interior plaster decorations, including the elaborate proscenium, are in good condition. A restored Parkway could provide a much-needed anchor for the fallow neighborhood around North Avenue and Charles Street. (Photograph courtesy of Thomas Paul.)

Keith's Theater (114 West Lexington Street) started out as the Garden in January 1915. It was designed by New York architect Thomas W. Lamb, who squeezed the 2,700-seat theater into an oddly-shaped lot. For many years, it presented vaudeville and movies. Keith's closed in 1955; the auditorium was demolished long ago for a parking lot, but the entrance building is still standing.

The Lincoln Theater (934–936 Pennsylvania Avenue) started life in 1916. It was a vaudeville and movie theater serving the African American population on lower Pennsylvania Avenue. Cab Calloway and Bessie Smith were two of the noted entertainers who appeared on the Lincoln's stage. It was razed in 1971.

This Belnord Theater (2700 Pulaski Highway) was built in 1921 on the site of an earlier theater. The Belnord was a large theater seating 1,200 people, including 479 in a spacious balcony. After it closed in 1969, the Belnord was used as a food market. (*News-American* photograph courtesy of Special Collections, University of Maryland Libraries.)

The Red Wing Theater (2239 East Monument Street) was the action house in the Jefferson neighborhood, while the nearby State Theater showed more sophisticated fare. The Red Wing was built on the site of Augie Pahl's earlier open-air theater in 1916 and lasted until 1960.

Architect Edward H. Glidden designed this neighborhood theater in the Italianate style for the Forest Park Motion Picture Company. The Forest (3300 Garrison Boulevard) opened in December 1919 and closed in May 1961. The building is still standing, but much of the front has been remodeled; it is used for religious purposes. (*News-American* photograph courtesy of Special Collections, University of Maryland Libraries.)

This impressive theater was planned as the Blue Bird Theater, but the name was changed before it opened. The 500-seat Rialto (846 West North Avenue) opened in June 1916 and closed in 1964. (*News-American* photograph courtesy of Special Collections, University of Maryland Libraries.)

During World War I, many anti-German movies were made. In Baltimore, feelings against Germany ran so high that German books were burned, German Street became Redwood Street, and some wanted the study of the German language banned in schools. In one East Baltimore movie theater, a man was locked up for disorderly conduct after he applauded a picture of the Kaiser.

All Next Week

TO HELL
WITH THE
KAISER

The Big Smashing Attraction Sensation of a Generation.

Featuring

MR. LAWRENCE GRANT

As the Kaiser with

OLIVE TELL and a cast of 12,000

With astounding realism portraying the lustful, remorseless avalanche of barbarism with which the Hun has cursed the world.

Showing what every American wants to see, THE TRUTH NAKED AND UNDRAPED.

Every heart in America will beat faster
Every hand in America will grip tighter
Every mind in America will see clearly
the supreme duty of the hour.

FIRST TIME IN BALTIMORE AT POPULAR PRICES.

Matinees until 6 P. M.   15c.
Evenings   25c.

INCLUDING THE WAR TAX.

The Wilson
BALTIMORE & GAY STS.

PHOTO PLAYS EXCLUSIVELY

DIRECTION OF

GUY L. WONDERS

WEEK OF SEPT. 23rd, 1918

ANNOUNCEMENT

On and after Monday, September 23rd, Admission prices will be—

Morning and afternoon until 6 P. M.

Children   10c.
Adults   15c.

Evenings

Children   15c.
Adults   20c.

INCLUDING THE WAR TAX.

ALL NEXT WEEK
"To Hell With The Kaiser"

One of the greatest theaters in the state, the 3,000-seat Century (18 West Lexington Street) was built for local impresario Charles Whitehurst in 1921. It was one of the first theaters designed by John J. Zink. After it was acquired by Loew's in the mid-1920s, John Eberson did the plans for a major remodeling and also designed a new theater, the Valencia, in the rooftop ballroom above the Century. The Century's huge marquee and vertical sign were dominant fixtures of the unit block of West Lexington Street until redevelopment wiped out the block in the 1960s. (Photograph courtesy of Don Gunther.)

Frank and Paul Hornig opened the first Horn Theater on West Pratt Street in September 1909. It was so successful that they tore it down and built a bigger theater on the site. The second Horn (2016 West Pratt Street) opened in 1920 and lasted until 1970. It is now operating as a church.

The Capitol Theater (1518 West Baltimore Street) was West Baltimore's entry in the movie palace building contest of the early 1920s. Seating about 1,200, it opened in February 1921 and lasted until 1970. It was converted into a factory in the mid-1970s.

Architect J. E. Moxley designed two theaters in Baltimore, the Columbia (709 Washington Boulevard) and the Westway at North Bend. The Columbia was certainly the better of these. Built for pioneer exhibitor Eugene McCurdy, the Columbia opened in November 1921. It lasted until the 1960s, when it was used as a church for a few years. In the summer of 1972, the Columbia was razed to clear the right-of-way for the new Martin Luther King Boulevard. (*News-American* photograph courtesy of Special Collections, University of Maryland Libraries.)

Baltimore architect Otto G. Simonson designed the Metropolitan (1524 West North Avenue) for Dr. Frederick Schanze's Metropolitan Theater Company. It seated 1,400 when it opened in December 1922. Better known as the "Met," this theater's claim to fame is that it was the site of the first successful sound movie exhibitions in the state. Warner Bros. Studios' *Don Juan* opened there in January 1927, and *The Jazz Singer* played at the Met a year later. The Met closed in 1977 and was torn down for a subway station in 1978. (Photograph courtesy of the Library of Congress, Motion Picture Division, LaFalce Exploitation Collection, Box G51.)

The first theater on this site was also called the Cluster. It opened in 1909 and lasted until 1921, when it was replaced by the present building. The second Cluster (303 South Broadway) opened in September 1921 and closed in 1982. The beautiful vertical sign, one of the last in the state, was removed by 1999. The Cluster was the second theater in Baltimore to show *The Jazz Singer*. It also boasted one of the first air-conditioning systems in town. The Cluster has been used as a church for several years.

The Royal Theater (1329 Pennsylvania Avenue) opened in 1922 as the Douglass Theater. Despite difficulties in its early years, it became a well-known venue for African American entertainers. Over the years, artists such as Count Basie, Fats Waller, Louis Armstrong, Jackie "Moms" Mabley, and Mamie Smith appeared on the Royal's stage.

The huge auditorium of the Royal stands empty here, waiting for the wreckers. The Royal closed in 1970 and was demolished in 1971, another victim of urban renewal in Baltimore.

The magnificent Stanley Theater (516 North Howard Street), built on the site of the Academy of Music, was the largest movie theater in the state. It was designed for the Stanley-Crandall Company by Philadelphia architects Hoffman and Henon. Seating 4,000 people in a luxurious setting usually reserved for Old World palaces and cathedrals, the Stanley opened in the fall of 1927. The huge lobby featured crystal chandeliers, historical murals, and several different kinds of imported marble. In its final years, the Stanley was called the Stanton. The dazzling, white facade of the Stanley fell to wreckers' machines in 1965; its size and beauty could not save it. (Photograph courtesy of Don Gunther.)

By one of those strange quirks of fate, the tiny Little Theater (523 North Howard Street), which seated a mere 238 people, opened across the street from the mighty 4,000-seat Stanley just three months after that giant had opened in September 1927. It was Baltimore's premiere art house for many years but ended its life in 1989 by showing pornographic films. It too was demolished to build a parking lot, the same fate the Stanley endured two decades earlier.

The State Theater (2045 East Monument Street) was the largest neighborhood theater in Maryland. It seated just over 2,000 people and was designed by two architects, George Schmidt and C. C. Fulton Leser. The State had a large stage and presented vaudeville shows until the 1950s. In 1936, an escaped lion raced through a startled audience before being captured in the theater's lobby. The State opened in 1927 and closed in 1963.

The Vilma (3403 Belair Road) was built by the Gaertner organization in 1928. It was designed by John Eyring in a style similar to his Strand Theater in Dundalk. The Vilma closed in 1973 and was turned into a catering hall. It is now a church.

The Edgewood Theater (3500 Edmondson Avenue) had one of John Zink's most beautiful fronts. It opened in October 1930. The Edgewood closed after a short life as an art theater in 1961. It has been used as a church for many years. The facade has been significantly remodeled, but it is still beautiful. (Photograph courtesy of Tom Kiefaber.)

The Edgewood's auditorium and proscenium were fine examples of a top neighborhood theater of the 1930s. John Zink designed both the Edgewood and Bridge theaters in 1930, but their auditoriums could not have been more different. (Photograph courtesy of Tom Kiefaber.)

The present-day condition of this theater belies its original spectacular interior design. The Bridge (2100 Edmondson Avenue) was designed by John Zink. It opened in March 1930 and lasted until 1968. It has been used as a church since 1970.

The art deco–style interior of the Bridge was one of the most beautiful in the state.

The Harlem Theater (614 North Gilmor Street) was built behind the granite facade of the Harlem Park Methodist Episcopal Church in 1932. The Harlem boasted one of the few atmospheric interiors among Maryland theaters. It closed in 1975 and was converted back into a church.

Probably the classiest neighborhood movie theater in the state, the beautiful Ambassador (4604 Liberty Heights Avenue) was designed for Durkee Enterprises by Baltimore architect John J. Zink. The Ambassador was one of Zink's most successful and exuberant designs. It seated just under 1,000 when it opened in September 1935. It lasted until 1968. It was converted into a skating rink and later a school. It sits empty now; hopefully, it will be restored to its former splendor someday.

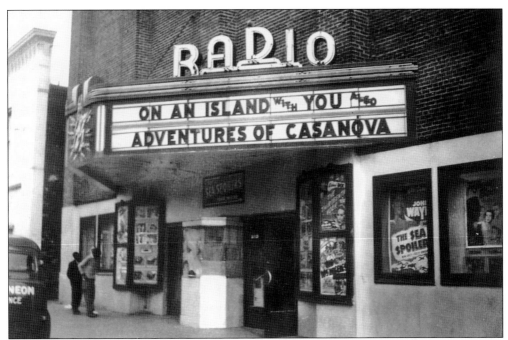

The Radio Theater (627 North Eden Street) was built within a large structure that had originally been an icehouse. Some longtime residents referred to it as the "Icehouse Theater." It opened in March 1938. The name was changed to the Star in 1944. It closed in 1957 and has been demolished.

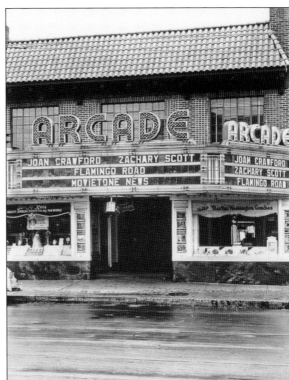

A long arcade led from Harford Road over a bridge to the Arcade auditorium (5436 Harford Road), which was located in a separate building. Durkee Enterprises opened the Arcade in 1928. It was designed by Oliver B. Wight and seated about 1,000 on one floor.

Baltimore's first newsreel theater, the Times (1711—1715 North Charles Street) opened in October 1939. It was built in one half of a large brick building that had originally been a powerhouse for the City Passenger Railway. In 1958, it was remodeled, and the name was changed to the Charles. Since the 1970s, the Charles has been one of the premier venues in Baltimore for independent films. In 1997, new owners remodeled the theater and added four auditoriums.

The Westway Theater (5300 Edmondson Avenue) opened in 1939 in the small commercial center at North Bend. After facing years of heavy competition from the Alpha, Edgewood, Westview, and Edmondson Village, it closed in 1978. It has been converted into a church. Architect J. E. Moxley's design for the Westway featured a unique, nearly circular marquee and free-standing ticket booth.

The Westport Theater (2305 Russell Street) served the Westport neighborhood between 1940 and 1957. Designed by E. Bernard Evander, it had an attractive art deco–style front that featured colored terra-cotta and glass bricks. Another Evander theater, the Waldorf (see page 83) is similar to the Westport.

The Patapsco Theater (601 Patapsco Avenue), which opened in September 1944, was one of the four movie theaters serving the Brooklyn and Curtis Bay neighborhoods. It was the last of the four to close when it ceased operation in 1977. The art deco–style building, designed by David Harrison, is still standing, minus the marquee.

Schwaber Theaters, an innovative Baltimore circuit, converted its Homewood Theater (9 West Twenty-fifth Street) into the Playhouse in 1951. The Playhouse was an art house, and over the next five years, Schwaber converted two other theaters into art houses. The film *Never on Sunday* played there for 45 weeks in 1960–1961. The Playhouse closed in 1985, and, despite several attempts to reopen it, it stands deserted.

The 800-seat Paramount Theater (6650 Belair Road) opened in October 1946. It closed in the fall of 1978 and has been converted into an office building. It was virtually identical to the Playhouse (pictured above), the Apex, and the Colgate.

The neo-Colonial architecture of the Edmondson Village Theater (4428 Edmondson Avenue) blends in with the adjoining Edmondson Village Shopping Center, one of the earliest shopping centers in Maryland. The theater was designed by Kenneth Cameron Miller. It opened in June 1949 and closed in 1974.

The oft-remodeled and, sadly, soon-to-be lost New Theater (210 West Lexington Street) was opened by local theatrical impresario Charles E. Whitehurst in 1910. It was designed as a vaudeville house by A. Lowther Forrest and Oliver B. Wight. The interior was gutted in 1945 and rebuilt in an art-deco style. The New was the scene of many local premieres; occasionally, the crowds blocked Lexington Street, as seen in this 1957 photograph when *The Ten Commandments* played there. (*News-American* photograph courtesy of Special Collections, University of Maryland Libraries.)

The Crest Theater (5425 Reisterstown Road) was certainly one of the most elegant movie theaters in Baltimore when it opened in February 1949. With 1,538 seats, it was also one of the largest single-screen theaters built in the state after World War II. It was located in the Hilltop Shopping Center a few doors from Mandell's Restaurant and across the street from the diner made famous in Barry Levinson's movie *Diner*. The Crest received an award for outstanding design.

A magnificent facade of white limestone; back-lit glass bricks; a huge, semi-circular marquee; and yards of neon graces the impressive Senator Theater (5904 York Road). The Senator was designed by John Zink for Durkee Enterprises; it opened in October 1939. One of the finest single-screen movie theaters in the nation, the Senator continues to provide first-run films to Baltimore audiences.

Two

BALTIMORE COUNTY

The first movies in Baltimore County were shown at Electric Park when it was still in the county. Early theaters were in Highlandtown before it was absorbed by Baltimore city. There were early exhibitions in Towson, Catonsville, and Dundalk. In Towson, movies were shown at church halls and at an open-air theater in 1915, and the tiny Recreation Theater opened on York Road in 1916. In St. Helena, the Community Church had movies in 1924. Caltrider's Hall in Reisterstown had movies around 1925. In 1917, movies were shown in Catonsville at the old high school on Frederick Avenue and at the Independent Order of Odd Fellows (IOOF) hall on Ingleside Avenue.

Larger theaters began appearing in the late 1920s: the Strand (Dundalk, 1927), the Alpha (Catonsville, 1928), and the Towson (Towson, 1928). The New Theater opened in Reisterstown in 1934. The Hollywood opened in Arbutus in 1936. After 1940, there was an increase in theater construction. The Aero opened in 1942 to serve workers at the Glenn L. Martin plant in Middle River. Later theaters opened in Edgemere (Edgemere, 1944), Middle River (Midway, 1945; and Hiway, 1946), Turner's Station (Anthony, 1945), Dundalk (Watersedge, 1947), and North Point (North Point Drive-In, 1948).

During the great era of drive-in theaters, when land was cheap, several opened in Baltimore County. In White Marsh, the General Pulaski opened in 1950, the Edmondson opened in Catonsville in 1954, the huge Timonium opened in 1955, the marvelous Bengies (the only currently operating drive-in in the state) opened in Middle River in 1956, and the Valley opened in Owings Mills in 1961. After 1960, most of the new theaters were built outside the city. Some notable theaters were the Cinema I and II in Lutherville (1964), the Westview in Catonsville (1965), the North Point Plaza in North Point (1966), and the Perring Plaza in Carney (1966).

The Cinema I and II in Lutherville made history as the first twin theater in the state. The trend for multi-screened theaters has continued up to the present. The last decade of the 20th century saw the opening of megaplexes clustered around huge new malls that dwarfed earlier shopping centers. In Baltimore County, there are the Valley Center 9 in Owings Mills (1990), the White Marsh 16 (1997), the Owings Mills Cinema 17 (1998), and the Hunt Valley Cinema 12 (in Cockeysville, 1998). The Eastpoint 10 (1995) in Dundalk was a link between multiplexes and megaplexes.

The Lyceum Theater (Fifth and D Streets, Sparrows Point) opened around 1912. It was a large-frame structure that seated nearly 600 patrons. The original entrance can be seen in this photograph, taken before 1921. (Photograph courtesy of William Hollifield.)

The Lyceum served the workers and their families at the huge Bethlehem steel works with movies, live shows, and graduations for 38 years, closing around 1950. This c. 1940 photograph shows the theater's modernized brick entrance. (Photograph courtesy of the Dundalk and Patapsco Neck Historical Society.)

This Strand (1309 Francis Avenue, Halethorpe) was one of many Strands in the state. It opened before 1925 and closed about 10 years later. The auditorium was located on the second floor of a hardware store operated by a Mr. Spindler.

Movies were shown at the Mount Washington Casino (South Avenue and First Street, Mount Washington) during the second decade of the 20th century. This attractive Queen Anne–style building was also used for summer theater and community events before it was razed in 1958.

The Strand (One Shipping Place, Dundalk), another of the Strands in the state, was the Dundalk area's second movie theater. The Community Church in nearby St. Helena predated it by about six years. The Strand operated between 1927 and 1985. This photograph shows the Strand around 1975.

The Strand was designed by John F. Eyring and was nearly a twin to his Vilma Theater on Belair Road, both on the outside and the inside. As shown here, every possible kind of prop was available to advertise a movie.

The Towson Theater (512 York Road, Towson) opened in March 1928. It lasted as a movie theater until 1992; it is still operating as a venue for live music shows. Much of the original facade remains above the marquee.

Fort Holabird, the small military base in Dundalk that was built as a motor-repair base in 1918, had a movie theater from the mid-1930s until the base closed in 1973. The theater has been demolished, and little remains of the U.S. Army Intelligence School that was located there for many years. The theater was the same 1932 design as the theater at Fort Howard; both seated 398. (Photograph courtesy of the Dundalk and Patapsco Neck Historical Society.)

The Aero Theater (1417 Fuselage Avenue, Middle River) was a product of World War II. It opened in May 1942 in the Aero Shopping Center, built to serve the workers at the nearby Glenn L. Martin plant. It closed in 1977. It was later torn down. (Photograph courtesy of the Library of Congress, Prints and Photographs Division, Office of War Information Collection, LC-USW3-036085-C.)

Catonsville's main movie theater for more than 30 years, the Alpha (725 Frederick Avenue) opened in March 1928 and closed in 1961. It received a new art deco–style facade in 1938 but retained its original uncomfortable wooden seats for many years. The basement bowling alleys provided thunderous accompaniment to the films shown there.

After the original Hollywood Theater (5509 Oregon Avenue, Arbutus) was destroyed by fire in 1995, it was replaced by a bigger, four-screen theater also called Hollywood. The first Hollywood Theater opened in September 1936 with *Call of the Wild*.

The second Hollywood opened in May 1998. The architects designed the new theater with a marquee and facade that is a near duplicate of the original theater.

The fight to save the 1938 Pikes Theater (1001 Reisterstown Road, Pikesville) lasted 13 years. When it was over in 1997, the groups that wanted to save the theater had lost. The Pikes was turned into an ethnic market that only lasted seven years. Fortunately, much of the beautiful art deco–style exterior of the theater is intact.

This attractive theater is still hanging on. The architectural firm Fenton and Lichtig designed the Hillendale (1045 Taylor Avenue, Hillendale) for Joseph Grant in 1960. It was the first new hardtop theater built in the state in the 1960s. The Hillendale was twinned in 1979 and closed in 1988. It has opened and closed several times since then. It would be nice to see a successful reopening for this theater.

Schwaber Theaters opened the attractive Cinema I and II Theater in the York Ridge Shopping Center in Lutherville in 1964. It was the first twin theater in the state. The name was changed to the Yorkridge 2 in 1979, and it was cut up into four theaters in 1983. It closed in January 2000 and was demolished four years later.

The original Westview (6023–6026 Baltimore National Pike, Catonsville) was one of the most spectacular movie theaters built in the state in the 1960s. It was designed by Fenton and Lichtig, and was located adjacent to the Edmondson Drive-In. The Westview opened in 1965. Sadly, it was cut up into several smaller theaters, and by the time it closed in 1997, it had morphed into a complex of 10 little theaters.

One of the many handsome, comfortable, single-screen theaters built by John Broumas, the North Point Plaza (2399 North Point Boulevard) languished from 1966 to 1998 in a small shopping center in North Point Village. It has been replaced by a big-box store.

JF Theaters opened the Village Theater (11900 Reisterstown Road, Reisterstown) in August 1966. With 900 seats, it was one of the big shopping-center theaters built in the 1960s that ringed the city. R/C Theaters acquired the theater in 1979. It was triplexed in 1985 and converted to a video store 12 years later.

Boasting one of the largest and prettiest auditoriums in the state behind a plain, unimposing facade and a row of uninspiring multiplex auditoriums, the Eastpoint 10 (7938 Eastern Avenue, Baltimore) is a largely unappreciated theater. It was designed by John Carroll Dunn for R/C Theaters and opened in 1995.

This huge megaplex adjacent to Owings Mills Mall seems to rival the Pentagon in size. It was built by General Cinemas in 1998 and seats around 3,000 people. The 64,000-square-foot Owings Mills Cinema 17 (10100 Mill Run Circle, Owings Mills) originally had three luxuriously appointed premium auditoriums with gourmet food and leather seats that were supposed to cater to patrons over the age of 21.

Hoyt's Theaters built several megaplexes in the Mid-Atlantic region in the late 1990s. The 12-screen theater behind the Hunt Valley Mall in Cockeysville opened in November 1998. It can seat about 2,500 people. It was acquired by Regal Theaters in 2003.

Three

CENTRAL MARYLAND
MONTGOMERY, CARROLL, HOWARD, AND ANNE ARUNDEL COUNTIES

Annapolis had the earliest movies in central Maryland. The earliest movie exhibition there was the one given by Thomas Armat at the Opera House in 1901. Tickets for the two-hour show cost between 25¢ and 50¢. Music between the movies was provided by a violinist and pianist from Washington, D.C. The exhibition, called a great success, consisted of short scenes that included the funeral of President McKinley and a yacht race. In 1906, there was a biographical exhibition at the Colonial Theater. The Maryland Avenue Methodist Church hosted early movie exhibitions, including the American Entertainment Company's "Lifephonetic Combination" of films and Prof. J. A. Loose's movies in 1907. The first movie theaters in Annapolis were clustered around the City Market (the Lyric and Burtis) or on Church Street (the Magnet and later the Republic). The large African American population in Annapolis supported two theaters, a converted hall on Clay Street and the Star Theater.

For many years, movie theaters in Montgomery County were concentrated in the county's Washington, D.C. suburbs. Rockville had a movie theater by 1915 when the Seco Theater opened. The first movie theater in Silver Spring, also called the Seco, opened in 1927. Bethesda's early movie theater was the Bethesda in 1928. It was renamed the State, then Hiser, and finally Baronet before it closed in 1977. An early movie exhibition in the county was at the Masonic hall in Gaithersburg around 1913. The Lyric Theater was built there several years later. The interesting Druid Theater, based on Washington's Apex Theater, opened in Damascus in 1947.

In Ellicott City, early movies were shown by Baltimore movie men Marion Pearce and Philip Scheck. The earliest movie theater was Edward Rodey's Amusea, which opened around 1912 in the old opera house building. In the mill town of Savage, the Baldwin Memorial Theater opened in 1921. Other movie theaters in Howard County were located in Elkridge, Columbia, and Oakland Mills. At the present time, Howard County is served by two 14-screen megaplexes, the United Artists theater at Snowden Square and the AMC theater at Columbia Mall.

Early movies in Carroll County were shown at the Opera House in Westminster. The Star Theater opened there around 1909. The Carroll opened in 1937 and has been beautifully restored as a performing arts center. There were movie theaters in Eldersburg, Hampstead, Manchester, Middleburg, New Windsor, Sykesville, Taneytown, Union Bridge, Westminster, and Woodbine. There were drive-ins near Westminster and Taneytown.

The Circle Playhouse (46 State Circle, Annapolis) opened in September 1920. It seated just under 1,000 people and was designed by Henry Powell Hopkins, who also designed the chapel at the University of Maryland, College Park. Hopkins matched the Colonial character of Annapolis's architecture in his design for the Circle. (Henry Powell Hopkins Papers' photograph courtesy of Special Collections, University of Maryland Libraries.)

This interior photograph of the Circle Theater shows the steep balcony characteristic of vaudeville houses. Note also the primitive air-conditioning machines on the side walls. (Henry Powell Hopkins Papers' photograph courtesy of Special Collections, University of Maryland Libraries.)

This image of the Circle Theater shows how it looked a few years before it closed. The theater closed in 1983, and after several attempts to save it, the theater was converted into an office building in 1993.

John J. Zink designed the New Glen Theater (130 Crain Highway, Glen Burnie) for Robert Gruver in 1941. The New Glen was intended to provide a modern theater for Glen Burnie as a replacement for the 10-year-old Glen Theater. The New Glen itself was doomed by the Harundale and Glen Burnie Mall theaters in the 1960s. It ended its run as an X-rated theater and was torn down as part of an urban renewal district. (Photograph courtesy of Lawrence H. Rushworth.)

The Republic Theater (187 Main Street, Annapolis) opened in 1915. In December 1922, it was gutted by a fire that started by an overheated furnace under the stage. It was quickly rebuilt and reopened in March 1923. Following an area-wide trend, the Republic was converted into an art house and was renamed the Playhouse.

The Playhouse closed in October 1980 with an appropriate film, *The Final Countdown*. An unsuccessful attempt was made in 1981 to reopen the theater as a concert hall. After that failed, the building was demolished.

The Plaza Theater (3002 Forest Drive, Parole) was designed for Durkee Enterprises by Mitchel Abramowitz; it seated nearly 900 people. It opened in Parole adjacent to the Colonial Drive-In in 1966. In 1975, it was altered into a 250-seat theater and a 600-seat theater. It closed in 1988. The building has been converted into a restaurant. In the photograph the drive-in's screen can be seen on the right side of the theater. (Photograph courtesy of the Baltimore Museum of Industry.)

The large, barn-like Liberty Theaters were built during World War I to provide venues for live shows and movies at military bases when large numbers of men were called up for service. This photograph shows a typical Liberty Theater located at Camp Meade. This theater opened in February 1918. (Photograph courtesy of the Fort Meade Museum.)

The Citizens Military Training Camp at Fort George G. Meade had an open-air movie theater. Although it was more elaborate, this open-air theater was similar to earlier open-air theaters in Baltimore and Washington, D.C. Open-air theaters were cheap to build and operate, but they were subject to the vicissitudes of summer weather. (Photograph courtesy of William Hollifield.)

Theater No. 1 (Llewelyn and Roberts Avenues, Fort George G. Meade) opened in 1933. It was one of the many movie theaters built on military posts in the 1930s. Although it was similar to the theaters at Fort Howard and Fort Holabird, Theater No. 1 was larger, seating 574. Of the six theaters operating at Fort Meade during World War II, this is the only one still showing films.

The Muvico Theater (7000 Arundel Mills Circle, Arundel Mills Mall, Harmans) with 24 screens is the largest megaplex in the state. Designed by the Development Design Group in an Egyptian style, the lobby has a blue-tile Nile River, statues of ancient Egyptian gods, and hieroglyphic-inscribed walls. Even the corridor and auditorium walls have scenes of ancient Egypt. The opening of this grand theater heralded a new age of flamboyance in theater design.

The Milo Theater (120 Commerce Lane, Rockville) was designed by John J. Zink and named after its owner, Rufus E. Milor. It opened in October 1935 and lasted until 1969. Sidney Lust operated it until 1955. The name was changed to the Villa in 1956. (Star Collection, reprinted by permission of the D.C. Public Library; © *Washington Post*.)

The Seco Theater (8242–8244 Georgia Avenue, Silver Spring) opened in November 1927. Seco was an acronym for the Southern Electric Company. It was designed by the architectural firm Faulconer and Proctor.

The Seco was acquired by the Roth organization in 1953. They made extensive changes and reopened it as Roth's Silver Spring. It closed in 1991 and is now a church.

Druid Clodfelter built the Druid Theater in Damascus in 1947 and named it after himself. It was designed by George Knott and based on John Zink's Apex Theater in Washington. In spite of a unanimous vote by the local historic preservation commission to have it designated as an historic structure, the Druid was gutted, leaving only the facade, in 1991.

One of the last theaters designed by John Zink's office, the Langley (8014 New Hampshire Avenue, Langley Park) was opened in a strip mall by KB Theaters in March 1952. The $300,000 theater with 987 seats was similar to Baltimore's Northwood Theater, which opened two years earlier. The Langley was cheaply twinned in 1982; it closed seven years later and is now a store.

The Roth organization built the Silver Spring East (951 Thayer Street, Silver Spring). The 383-seat theater was built in what had been an ice-skating rink. It lasted from November 1969 until 1988.

This theater had four names during its nearly 50-year history. It opened as the Bethesda (7414 Wisconsin Avenue, Bethesda) in November 1928. The name was changed to the State about a year later when Henry Hiser took it over. Hiser renamed the theater after himself in 1939. The Hiser was acquired by KB Theaters in 1960. KB changed the name to Baronet and operated it until it closed in 1977. It has been demolished and was replaced by the Bethesda Metro station. (Photograph courtesy of the Library of Congress, Prints and Photographs Division, Joseph S. Allen Collection, LC-A7-3096.)

The Bethesda Theater (7719 Wisconsin Avenue, Bethesda), which opened as the Boro in 1938, had one of the nicest facades in the area before new construction behind it ruined it. It was one of the theaters designed for Sidney Lust by John Eberson. It became the Bethesda Cinema 'n Drafthouse in 1983 and closed in 2001. It reopened as a legitimate theater in the fall of 2007. (Photograph courtesy of Paul Sanchez.)

The Viers Mill Theater (12202 Viers Mill Road, Silver Spring) sported the trademark comedy and tragedy masks of the Sidney Lust organization. It was designed by Richard L. Parli and showed films between 1950 and 1975. It has been remodeled into a drugstore. (Photograph courtesy of the Library of Congress, Prints and Photographs Division, Horydczak Collection, LC-H814-2631-001.)

The American Film Institute took a beat-up neighborhood theater and polished it until it shone like a jewel in downtown Silver Spring. The Silver (8606 Colesville Pike, Silver Spring) opened in September 1938. It was an art deco–style design by master theater architect John Eberson. A bitter fight over the preservation of the Silver resulted in the destruction of the original marquee tower and tile mosaics, but after several years of negotiations, the restored theater reopened in 2003.

KB Theaters opened the Flower Avenue Playhouse (8725 Flower Avenue, Silver Spring) in February 1950. After KB closed it in 1979, Paul Sanchez acquired it and reopened it as a twin theater in September 1980. Two small auditoriums were added adjacent to the original theater in 1983. The Flower closed in 1996. After an unsuccessful attempt to preserve it as a theater, it has been converted into a church.

The Kentlands Theater (629 Centerpoint Way, Gaithersburg), one of the new megaplexes of the 1990s, opened in December 1998. It seats 1,200 patrons in eight auditoriums. The Kentlands Theater is one of the few new theaters in the state that was built by a local, independent exhibitor, and its pleasing, unique, ultra-modern design emphasizes this difference.

Dripping with neon and seating more than 2,000 people, Silver Spring's newest megaplex dominates the new shopping center at Fenton and Ellsworth Streets. The Majestic is typical of the new breed of movie theaters, announcing its presence with bright lights and a massive facade. It opened in May 2004.

The Carroll Baldwin Memorial Community Hall in the small mill town of Savage in southern Howard County was dedicated as a library and recreation center in November 1922. This attractive stone building, located on the southeast corner of Baltimore and Foundry Streets, has served several functions, including as a movie theater, during its lifetime. Movies were shown there between 1923 and 1947.

The Columbia Palace 9 (8805 Centre Park Drive, Columbia) lasted only 15 years, from 1986 to 2001. It was too a short life for this attractive theater, which was designed by the architectural firm Kelly, Clayton, and Mojzisek.

The Snowden Square 14 megaplex (9161 Commerce Center Drive, Columbia) was opened in December 1997 by United Artists. The coming of this huge complex was a major factor in the closing of the Columbia City and Columbia Palace 9 theaters.

The AMC 14-screen megaplex is located next to the mall in Columbia. It was opened by the AMC organization in December 2003 and happily continues the trend toward glitzier movie theaters with its brightly lit, multi-story, glass facade.

The Carroll Theater (91 West Main Street, Westminster) opened in November 1939. It was designed by Baltimore architect Oliver B. Wight to seat 840 people. By the time this photograph was taken, the traditional triangular marquee had been removed from the front of the theater, and the interior had been twinned. After it closed in the late 1980s, it was converted into a church. In 2004, thanks to a farsighted Westminster City Council, a grant from the state, and the hard work of the Carroll County Arts Council, the renovated theater was reopened as the Carroll Arts Center.

The Rendezvous Theater (1340 Main Street, Hampstead) opened in 1947. After it closed c. 1965, it was converted into a church. Hampstead had three other theaters. The Central, which operated from the 1930s until 1955, is now used as an antiques mall. The Dreamland operated around 1915, and the Leister showed films in the mid-1920s. (Photograph by and courtesy of Herbert Harwood Jr.)

Four

SOUTHERN MARYLAND
PRINCE GEORGE'S, CHARLES, ST. MARY'S, AND CALVERT COUNTIES

The absence of any large cities in southern Maryland removed fertile ground for theaters, so most of the theaters came late and were small. As in Montgomery County, the largest concentration of early theaters was in the Washington, D.C., suburbs of Prince George's County in Hyattsville, Mount Rainier, and Capitol Heights. One of the earliest movie theaters in this area was the Red Wing in Laurel, which was operating as early as 1914. The Red Wing burned in 1928 and was replaced by Sidney Lust's Laurel Theater, which is still in use. Hyattsville and neighboring Riverdale had early nickelodeon theaters, but they did not last long. Two of the first modern movie theaters in the Washington, D.C., suburbs were the Cameo in Mount Rainier and the Arcade in Hyattsville.

The earliest movies in Calvert County were probably shown at the town hall in Prince Frederick, where films were being regularly shown by 1919. Later movies were shown in the Parish Hall in Solomons, and the D and L Theater opened in 1947. There was also an open-air theater in St. Leonard during the summer of 1944.

There was a "picture theater" in Leonardtown, St. Mary's County, as early as 1914. Films were shown in the Leonardtown Town Hall in the 1920s. Interestingly, the town hall auditorium, which seated around 225 people, was open only on Sunday nights. This would make it one of the earliest venues for Sunday movies in the state. During the big controversy in the 1930s when Baltimore finally got Sunday movies, a writer to the *Evening Sun* claimed that St. Mary's County had enjoyed Sunday-night movies for 25 years.

Charles County had movies at the YMCA in Indian Head by 1921. The Recreation Hall at Indian Head also showed movies in the mid-1920s. The Glymount Theater opened in 1936 and operated into the 1950s. Hughesville and La Plata had movie theaters by the mid-1930s. In 1940, two new movie theaters opened in the county. The Waldorf opened in Waldorf in mid-September 1940, and the Charles opened in La Plata later that same month.

The Laurel Academy of Music (northeast corner of Route 1 and Prince George Street, Laurel) was built in 1879; it was designed and built by L. A. Ellis. In 1915, the building was remodeled to include a garage on the ground floor, certainly one of the oddest combinations in the state. The life of the theater-garage was cut short by fire, which destroyed the structure in April 1917. The name lived on in the name of the car dealership erected on the site, Academy Ford.

The Laurel (314 Main Street, Laurel) opened in late 1929, replacing the Red Wing, which had burned a year earlier. It was designed for Sidney Lust by Harry Brandt. After it closed as a movie theater, it was used for a number of years as a dinner theater. (Photograph courtesy of Paul Sanchez.)

W. B. Spire's Arcade Theatre Corporation built the Arcade Theater (4318 Gallatin Street, Hyattsville); it was one of the first modern movie theaters built in the Washington, D.C., suburbs. The Arcade opened in November 1925. It was designed by John J. Carey and seated about 400 people. In this 1936 photograph, a children's show has just let out. The considerably remodeled shell of the Arcade still stands in downtown Hyattsville. (Photograph courtesy of Paul Sanchez.)

The Cameo Theater (3820 Thirty-fourth Street, Mount Rainier), which replaced an earlier open-air theater also called the Cameo, served Mount Rainier from 1924 until 1951. The Cameo building contained Dr. W. B. Spire's drugstore and a U.S. Post Office. The theater has been converted to a church. (Photograph courtesy of Paul Sanchez.)

John Eberson designed the Marlboro Theater (134 Main Street, Upper Marlboro) for Sidney Lust. It opened in January 1938 to serve the Prince George's County seat. The short-lived Marlboro lasted only 14 years, closing in 1952. The building was used as a newspaper office for many years. (Photograph courtesy of Paul Sanchez.)

The growing population of the old Washington, D.C., suburb of Hyattsville prompted exhibitor Sidney Lust to replace his 350-seat Arcade Theater with this 900-seat art deco–style beauty. The Hyattsville Theater (5612 Baltimore Boulevard) was designed by master theater architect John Eberson; it opened in November 1939 and entertained audiences until 1965. It was demolished to provide additional space for a car dealer. Now a townhouse development has risen on the site. (Photograph courtesy of Paul Sanchez.)

Nestled in a small shopping center in the middle of Old Greenbelt, the Greenbelt (129 Centerway, Greenbelt) is an undiscovered gem. It was built in 1938 to serve the New Deal planned community. A replacement sign duplicating the original was installed in 2000. The Greenbelt is still going strong. (Photograph courtesy of the Library of Congress, Prints and Photographs Division, Office of War Information Collection, LC-USW3-003454-C.)

Sidney Lust opened his Beltsville Drive-In on Baltimore Boulevard in July 1947. It was designed by George Peterson and covered 11 acres. It entertained many carloads of fans for 40 years, finally closing in 1987. The site of the drive-in is now covered by a strip mall. (Photograph courtesy of Paul Sanchez.)

The Cheverly Theater (5400 Landover Road, Cheverly) was designed for Sidney Lust by world-renowned architects John and Drew Eberson in 1947. After it closed in 1971, it was acquired by the Prince George's County government. (Photograph courtesy of Paul Sanchez.)

The Cheverly reopened as the Publick Playhouse in February 1977 and serves as the county's performing arts center. It was one of the first attempts in Maryland to restore and reuse a movie theater.

Sidney Lust opened the Hillside Drive-In (5210 Marlboro Pike, Coral Hills) in August 1953. It was designed by Ted Rogvoy. The opening night was a disaster; the sound system failed, and electrical problems caused a flood in the snack bar and toilets.

The men here in the opening ceremony—including Sidney Lust (left) and "Uncle" Dave Ginsburg, who is removing the barricade—do not seem to realize that chaos is just ahead. Despite its terrible opening, the Hillside lasted for 35 years.

The handsome Allen Theater (6822 New Hampshire Avenue, Takoma Park) opened in March 1951 at one end of a small shopping center. The 946-seat theater had spectacular neon signage, but some of it could not be used because the county thought it would be too distracting to motorists on New Hampshire Avenue. It was twinned in 1985 and closed in 1990. It is now a clothing store. (Photograph courtesy of Paul Sanchez.)

Kenneth Duke opened the Rex Theater in December 1941 as the St. Mary's Theater to replace his Duke Theater. It became the New in the late 1940s and lasted into the 1970s. It closed under the name of the Rex and was converted into a restaurant.

The Kaywood Theater (2211 Varnum Street, Mount Rainier) was one of the many movie theaters built around Baltimore and Washington, D.C., in the years immediately after World War II. It was built by Sidney Lust, one of the major theater builders in the suburban Washington, D.C., area, in 1945. The Kaywood lasted until 1977. It could seat nearly 1,000 patrons and featured a glass-enclosed nursery and special restroom and shower facilities for the theater staff. The building has been used as a church since the 1970s.

In the 1970s, the Roth organization converted several buildings in suburban Maryland into small movie theaters. This tiny one (375 seats) that served College Park was built in a former furniture store (7242 Baltimore Boulevard). It was demolished in 1994. A restaurant occupies the site now. (Photograph by and courtesy of Sarah C. Headley.)

The attractive Belair Theater (3315 Superior Lane, Bowie) lasted only 15 years, from 1966 to 1981, a short life for this large, well-designed theater. Sadly, many of the big beautiful theaters built in the 1960s have disappeared, rendered obsolete by the new multiplex theaters. The Belair still stands with few external changes.

The long-closed Riverdale Plaza Theater (5617 Riverdale Road, Riverdale) is a beautiful example of a 1960s movie theater. It seated just over 800 when it opened in March 1968. It was designed by Donald N. Coupard and Associates. It was twinned in 1993 and closed in 2001. The theater is still standing. It is one of the last of its kind.

One of the great single-screen movie theaters built in the 1960s, the Andrews Manor (4801 Allentown Road, Camp Springs) lasted just over 30 years, from 1965 to 1996. It was opened by the Broumas organization in May 1965. Like so many other large theaters—it boasted 880 seats—it was twinned in the 1980s. The building has become a furniture store, but externally, it has changed little.

Oddly enough, two movie theaters opened in the same month in Charles County. Both the Waldorf in Waldorf and the Charles in La Plata opened in September 1940. There were also movie theaters in Hughesville, Indian Head (the Recreation Hall and the Glymount), and Rock Point. Early films were shown at the YMCA in Indian Head and at the town hall in La Plata. Note the similarity between the Waldorf and the Westport (page 41). (Photograph courtesy of Paul Sanchez.)

The first movies shown in Solomons were probably those shown at the Parish Hall. In April 1947, the exhibitor Charles O. Dowell announced that he was ending his movies at the Parish Hall and opening a modern theater at the new D and L Shopping Center. (Photograph courtesy of the Calvert Marine Museum, Solomons, Maryland.)

Dowell and Laningham built the D and L Shopping Center one mile north of Solomons. It opened in June 1947 and contained Fowler's grocery store, the Tog Toggery Shop, a movie theater, and a snack bar. The theater was later renamed the Solomons Cinema. (Photograph courtesy of the Calvert Marine Museum, Solomons, Maryland.)

Five

WESTERN MARYLAND
FREDERICK, WASHINGTON, ALLEGANY, AND GARRETT COUNTIES

Three of the largest cities in Maryland—Cumberland, Hagerstown, and Frederick—are located in western Maryland. Each one had a large theater before the days of movies. In Cumberland, there were two: the Academy of Music and the Maryland Theater; Hagerstown also had an Academy of Music, and Frederick had the City Hall Opera House.

Cumberland had movies as early as January 1898 when there was a projectoscope exhibition at the Academy of Music, and a small movie theater opened there in May 1906. Cumberland was one of the few cities in Maryland that supported separate African American movie theaters. The 500-seat Howard Theater, which opened on North Mechanic Street in July 1927, was one of the largest African American theaters in the state. Allegany County's movie theaters were located in Barton, Cresaptown, Cumberland, Eckhart Mines, Frostburg, Lavale, Lonaconing, Luke, McCoole, Midland, Mount Savage, and Westernport. Recently, the 1931 art deco–style Embassy Theater was restored and reopened in downtown Cumberland. In Frostburg, the ancient Palace Theater is still operating. Mount Savage had movies as early as 1909.

Movies seem to have had a difficult time getting started in Hagerstown. There was one movie theater there, the Wizard, around 1908, and the Family Theater, was open by 1910. In the middle of that decade, two large theaters—the Colonial and Maryland—opened on South Potomac Street. The Maryland has been restored and has one of the most beautiful auditoriums in the state. The first multiplex theater in Washington County—a 16-screen, 2,700-seat complex at Valley Mall—opened in 2000. Other theater locations in Washington County include Boonsboro, Clear Spring, Hancock, Lavale, and Williamsport. Boonsboro had a movie house as early as 1910.

The first movies in Frederick were probably those shown at the City Opera House in 1897. A movie theater, the Marvel, opened there in 1911. A year later, the Empire opened. Frederick's movie palace, the Tivoli, opened in 1927. Movies were shown in the auditorium at Braddock Heights as early as 1904. Movie theaters were opened in Thurmont, Brunswick, Emmittsburg, Middletown, and Woodsboro. Most of these have disappeared, but the attractive Memorial Hall in Middletown is still in excellent condition.

Garrett County had movie theaters in Deer Park, Friendsville, Kitzmiller, and Oakland. Most of these theaters have also been destroyed. Early movies were shown in Kitzmiller by 1908 and in Oakland by 1910.

The City Hall Opera House (North Market Street, Frederick) reopened in the rear of the city hall building in November 1907. The 1,300-seat theater was designed by Martinsburg, West Virginia, architect George D. Whitson.

Baltimore exhibitors Marion Pearce and Philip Scheck leased the City Hall Opera House in 1909 and operated it as a movie and vaudeville house. It lasted until the 1950s. The building has been completely remodeled.

Farmers & Mechanics Bank, Empire Theatre and City Hall, Frederick, Md.

The Empire Theater (140 North Market Street, Frederick) opened in the Junior Fire Company Hall in September 1912. Four months later, plans were prepared by architect B. Evard Kepner to convert the hall into a modern, up-to-date movie theater. The new Empire opened in July 1913 and lasted well into the 1920s.

A huge crowd attended the opening ceremonies for the new Memorial Hall in Middletown, Frederick County, on May 27, 1923. It was designed by York, Pennsylvania, architect Edward Leber as a memorial to local men who served in World War I. The hall was a multi-purpose building for stage shows and movies. It replaced the 1904 City Hall Opera House around the corner on Church Street. By 1955, the hall had become a white elephant, and most of the members of the Memorial Hall Commission had died. In February 1955, the hall was sold to the Middletown Valley Grange.

The 300-seat State Theater (Main Street, Thurmont) operated between the mid-1930s and the mid-1950s. Movies were also shown at the Thurmont Town Hall and the Gem Theater in the early 1920s. (Photograph by and courtesy of Herbert Harwood Jr.)

The Holiday Cinema (100 Baughman's Lane, Frederick) opened next to the Holiday Inn in October 1969. It seated about 600 people and featured rocking chair lounger seats and a private screening room for parties. It has been operating as a discount theater for a number of years.

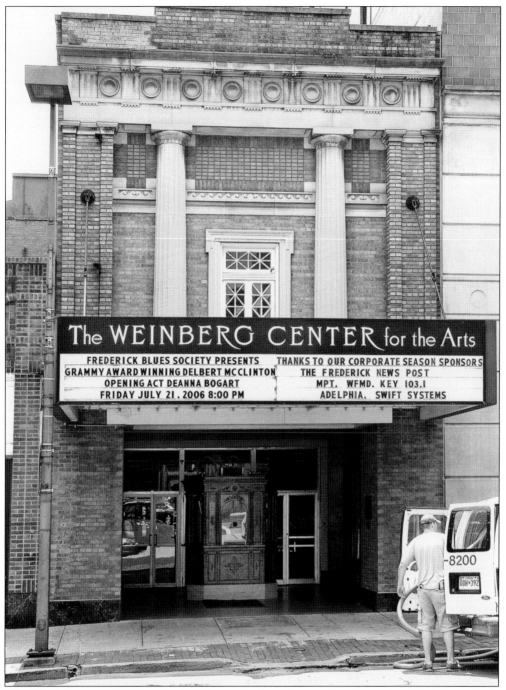

The Tivoli Theater (20 West Patrick Street, Frederick) opened in December 1926. It was built by the Stanley-Crandall Company and designed by John Zink. The 1,500-seat theater contained $15,000 worth of marble and more than half a million bricks made by the Frederick Brick Works, which also supplied bricks for the Episcopal Cathedral and Union Station in Washington, D.C. It closed in 1959 and was flooded twice before reopening as the Weinberg Center for the Performing Arts in 1978.

The Hoyt Cinema Corporation built this 10-screen, 1,875-seat multiplex in the remodeled Frederick Towne Mall on West Patrick Street in 1996. Like so many earlier multiplexes, it is hidden within an enclosed mall. The Frederick Towne Mall 10 replaced the twin theaters that had previously operated in the mall.

R/C Theaters of Reisterstown opened this imposing 16-screen megaplex in the Westview Promenade on Buckeystown Pike near Frederick in November 2003. Compare this theater with its bold conspicuous facade with Hoyts, which has so little exterior signage that it is difficult to find.

World-renowned theater architect Thomas Lamb designed this Maryland Theater (19 South Potomac Street, Hagerstown). It opened in May 1915. The original entrance was through the middle of the apartment building. The apartments were destroyed by fire in 1924, which spared the auditorium. Elaborate plaster decorations grace the box seats and proscenium arch of the Maryland. In the spring of 1928, it had the first installation of the Vitaphone sound system outside of Baltimore. (Photograph courtesy of William Hollifield.)

MARYLAND THEATRE, HAGERSTOWN, MD.

The roots of Henry's Theater (7 South Potomac Street, Hagerstown) go back to the Palace Theater in 1908. It was named for Henry Weinberg, who took the Palace over, renovated it, and reopened it in February 1931. Weinberg operated it until 1948. The theater closed in late 1979. The Elks Club Building where the theater was located is now being studied as the site for the Barbara Ingram School for the Arts.

Three movie theaters were clustered on South Potomac Street in Hagerstown. The Colonial Theater at 14 South Potomac was opened in 1914. By far the most spectacular part of the theater was the beautiful facade that featured a colorful terra-cotta sculpture at its apex. The Colonial closed in the 1950s. For a while, it was the home of country music shows, but it has now been converted into a church.

Almost any city worth its salt had an Academy of Music. The one in Hagerstown (44 West Washington Street) opened in October 1880 and closed around 1955. Hagerstown's Academy was designed by J. Crawford Neilson, who had designed Baltimore's Academy of Music five years earlier. The 600-seat theater was constructed during the rebuilding of the Washington House Hotel, which was destroyed by fire in May 1879.

The present San Toy Theater (48 Main Street, Lonaconing) was opened by the Evans Brothers in the fall of 1926, but an earlier San Toy was operating in Lonaconing a decade earlier. The first San Toy was destroyed by fire in the fall of 1923. Before they had the San Toy, the Evans Brothers operated the Evans Opera House in Lonaconing. The San Toy lasted until 1970. The building is still standing. The name San Toy, which has been used for mines and towns, probably originated as the name of a popular operetta written in 1899. The term is also Cockney rhyming slang for "boy."

The Maryland Theater (25 North Mechanic Street, Cumberland) opened with *The Gingerbread Man* on November 21, 1907. Philadelphia architect John D. Allen designed the $100,000 theater. Allen's company also prepared plans for James Kernan's Auditorium Theater in Baltimore in 1905. The 1,400-seat Maryland was operated by the Philadelphia-based Nixon and Zimmerman organization headed by Fred G. Nixon Nirdlinger. Prof. Charles E. Cope's 12-member orchestra provided the music.

The 1,400-seat Strand Theater (25–29 South Liberty Street, Cumberland) was the last of the great Cumberland movie theaters to be demolished. It was built for the Washington, D.C.-based Harry Crandall organization and opened on September 3, 1920. The Strand closed exactly 52 years to the date after it opened. Robert Slote, an early manager of the Strand, built a successful sound-on-disk system that was tried out at the Strand in 1928. (Photograph courtesy of the Allegany County Historical Society Photograph Collection, Record Group 12, Brooke Whiting Archives, Cumberland, Maryland, 2006/2.)

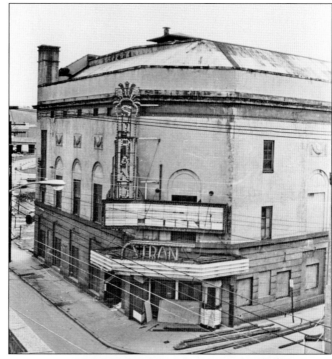

Children with chickens help advertise the film *The Egg and I* at Cumberland's Strand Theater in 1947. Contests like this and the big "COOL" sign hanging from the marquee are just two of the things missing from today's movie houses. (This photograph is part of the Herman and Stacia Miller collection and has been printed courtesy of the mayor and city council of Cumberland, Maryland.)

The Palace (33 East Union Street, Frostburg) dates back to 1906 when the Dreamland opened on the site. Six years later, a larger auditorium was added, and the name was changed to the Palace. The Palace served Frostburg until it closed in 1981. Through a combination of farsighted residents, sympathetic owners, and clever fundraising, the Palace was saved and purchased by a nonprofit group in 1987.

The beautiful, little Lyric Theater (24 South Main Street, Frostburg) was seriously damaged by fire in May 1921. It was rebuilt and operated well into the 1950s. Andy Thumser, advertised on the boards, was a well-known performer in Maryland theaters. He died in Baltimore in 1971. (This photograph is part of the Herman and Stacia Miller Collection and has been printed courtesy of the mayor and city council of Cumberland, Maryland.)

The Potomac Drive-In opened on Winchester Road near Cresaptown in August 1948. Admission was 60¢ per person; children under 12 in cars were admitted free. The Potomac Drive-In was the first drive-in in western Maryland. It closed around 1981. (Photograph courtesy of the Allegany County Historical Society Photograph Collection, Record Group 12, Brooke Whiting Archives, Cumberland, Maryland, 2006/2.)

The Starlite Drive-In was located on Oldtown Road; it opened in 1955. In 1968, the name was changed to Super 51 Drive-In. It closed in 1981. (Photograph courtesy of the Allegany County Historical Society Photograph Collection, Record Group 12, Brooke Whiting Archives, Cumberland, Maryland, 2006/2.)

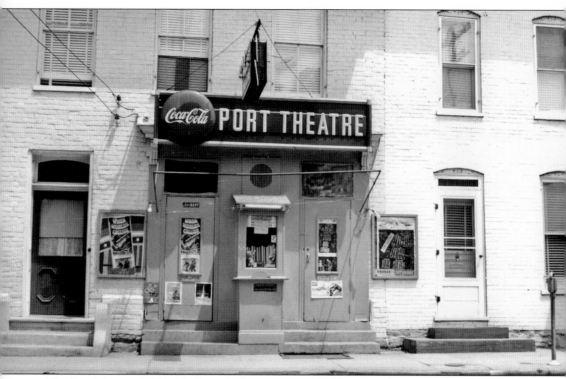

The Port Theater (17 North Conococheague Street, Williamsport) was earlier called the State. The name was changed to the Port around 1957. There was also an opera house in Williamsport and movie theaters called the New, Princess, and Pastime.

Six

NORTHEAST MARYLAND
HARFORD AND CECIL COUNTIES

It has not been possible to determine where the first movies were shown in northeast Maryland. Early films were exhibited in Elkton on the second floor of the Independent Order of Odd Fellows (IOOF) hall. In Bel Air, movies were shown at the Masonic temple as early as 1908. The City Opera House in Havre de Grace also had movies by 1908. Havre de Grace was the largest city in this area and had two small movie theaters, the Willou and the Bijou, both on St. John Street, by 1908. The first movie house in Bel Air was the Busy Moon, which opened around 1910. In the first two decades of the 1900s, several new movie houses were built, including the AACO (which stands for the Aberdeen Amusement Company) in Aberdeen, the Argonne in Bel Air, the Pen-Mar in Cardiff, the State in Havre de Grace, the Community Playhouse in Elkton, the Riverside in Port Deposit, and the movie theater at the Perry Point Explosives Depot. The large U.S. Naval Training Center at Bainbridge near Port Deposit also had a theater. In the early 1920s, Havre de Grace had one venue, an open-air theater on Girard Street, for African American audiences. African American patrons could also see movies at Johnnie's Sports Arena (1950–1968) in Darlington, where films were shown on Monday nights. Military theaters existed at the Aberdeen Proving Grounds and the Edgewood Arsenal, and a company theater was formerly located in the Bata Shoe factory at Belcamp. The Bel Air Drive-in, a relic of the 1950s, in Churchville had a long life from 1953 to 2005.

A local group in Bel Air tried hard to save the 1928 Bel Air Theater (earlier the Argonne Theater) in the 1980s but was not able to generate enough support, and the theater building was converted into office space. The major theaters in this area today are the small multiplex in Churchville and the 14-screen Regal megaplex in Abingdon.

The IOOF hall (114–118 North Street, Elkton), also known as the Opera House, was one of the earliest venues for movies in Cecil County. This building was built by the Odd Fellows organization in 1867. Movies were shown in the hall on the second floor as early as 1908. The last films were shown there in the late 1920s. The interior has been completely remodeled.

As early as 1908, the City Opera House on Union Avenue in Havre de Grace was presenting movies and vaudeville shows. In the spring of 1917, it was remodeled into a movie theater with a new asbestos projection booth and a Wonder screen. The programs consisted of a feature film, a comedy or "scenic," and an edition of the Pathe Weekly newsreel.

The Havre de Grace City Opera House burned before 1921, but it was rebuilt and showed films as late at 1929 when it was leased by Durkee Enterprises. The much-remodeled building remains.

The Elkton Community Playhouse opened in a multipurpose building on Main Street at the foot of North Street in October 1923. In addition to the 675-seat theater, the building contained a cafe and hotel. By 1930, the name had been changed to the New Theater. A devastating fire in December 1947 destroyed the theater and much of the surrounding area on the south side of Main Street. (Photograph courtesy of the Historical Society of Cecil County.)

The small Perry Point Theater was constructed in 1918 by the U.S. Army Ordnance Department to serve the new Atlas Powder Company's plant near Perryville on the banks of the Susquehanna River in Cecil County. The New York architectural firm Mann and MacNeille designed the theater and the surrounding new town of Perry Point for the workers at the powder plant. (Photograph courtesy of the Library of Congress, Prints and Photographs Division, Army Ordnance Department Collection, Lot 3936.)

Perry Point contained more than 300 houses, dormitories, a firehouse, stores, and a church. By the time this photograph was taken, the theater looked more like a movie house. (Photograph courtesy of the Historical Society of Cecil County.)

The North East Theater (Main Street, North East) opened in the mid-1930s and closed in the mid-1950s. It replaced the old opera house where movies had been shown since the early 1920s. (Photograph courtesy of the Historical Society of Cecil County.)

There were two adjacent movie theaters on St. John Street in Havre de Grace when the first Willou Theater opened in J. W. Bauer's harness shop in 1908. Bauer purchased the Bijou next to his Willou Theater in 1919 and remodeled it into a newer and bigger Willou (pictured), which opened in April 1920. The Willou was replaced by a new theater, the State, in 1927.

Baltimore-based exhibitor Durkee Enterprises opened the 500-seat State at 327 St. John Street in Havre de Grace in September 1927. It was built on the site of the old Willou Theater.

The State closed around 1960, but it was reopened for a short time in the 1980s. It has been converted into a church, but much of the theater's original facade remains.

POST THEATRE   EDGEWOOD ARSENAL, MARYLAND

The army's installation of the Edgewood Arsenal in Harford County included a motion picture theater similar to those at Fort Holabird and Fort Howard. It was built in the 1930s according to plans by the Office of the Quartermaster General. It could seat about 400 people.

The Joppatown Cinema (1024 Joppa Farm Road, Joppatown) was opened in July 1970 by JF Theaters. This 650-seat theater, designed by John W. Lawrence, was one of the most modern theaters in the state when it opened. It lasted 16 years. It closed in 1986 and has been completely remodeled. (Photograph courtesy of Don Gunther.)

Located on a large tract of land with abundant parking between two warehouse stores from which it is separated by rapidly disappearing blocks of forest, the Bel Air Cinema 14 (409 Constant Friendship Boulevard, Abingdon) opened in July 1997. At the time, the 3,000-seat Cinema 14 claimed to be the largest movie theater complex in Maryland. The facade of the theater is a variation of the familiar facade used for other Regal theaters, including the one in Sterling, Virginia.

The AACO Theater, which stands for Aberdeen Amusement Company, opened in 1919 on West Bel Air Avenue in Aberdeen. It was designed by Baltimore architect William O. Sparklin. The ice cream store next to the theater's entrance was a common adjunct to early movie theaters before the advent of interior concession stands. It was called the New by 1930 and closed in the late 1960s.

Seven

EASTERN SHORE
KENT, QUEEN ANNE, CAROLINE, TALBOT, DORCHESTER, WICOMICO, WORCESTER, AND SOMERSET COUNTIES

Most towns on the Eastern Shore had a venue for movies; the larger ones, Salisbury, Cambridge, Easton, Pocomoke City, Ocean City, and Crisfield, had several. The theaters there suffered terribly from fires. The theater in Ridgely burned three times. Arson was suspected, and guards were posted to prevent further fires. Crisfield lost the Arcade and Lyric to fire in 1928. Fire destroyed Salisbury's Arcade Theater in 1946, and the Ulman Theater there burned twice, in 1941 and in 1945. The Capitol Theater in Ocean City burned in 1964. The 1907 Opera House in Centreville burned in 1968. On the other hand, the Eastern Shore has fared fairly well in theater preservation. The Mar-Va in Pocomoke City, the Lyceum in Chestertown, the Avalon in Easton, the Globe in Berlin, and the Church Hill Theater in Church Hill have all been saved.

Kent County had theaters in Chestertown, Betterton, Tolchester, Millington, and Rock Hall. Rock Hall had an Amusea Theater by 1909. L. Bates showed movies in Stam's Hall (later called the Lyceum) in Chestertown around the same time. Paul Comegys showed films at his hall in Millington in the 1910s. In Queen Anne's County, there were movie theaters in Church Hill, Centreville, Grasonville, Queenstown, and Stevensville. The beautiful, little, art deco–style Church Hill Theater was saved from demolition in 1985.

Movie theaters were scattered around Caroline County, notably in Denton, Ridgely, and Federalsburg, but none have been saved. Talbot County's movie theaters were located in Easton, St. Michael's, Oxford, and Tilghman. The Avalon in Easton, home of several world premieres, reopened as a performing arts center in 1990. Dorchester County had theaters in Cambridge, Hurlock, and Fishing Creek. Cambridge had some of the earliest movie theaters on the Eastern Shore. The White House Theater and the Cambridge Picture Parlor operated there in 1908.

Crisfield in Somerset County had several early theaters, including the Lyric, Majestic, and Opera House. Lawson's Hall was listed as a movie theater by 1909. By the late 1920s, Princess Anne also had several theaters. Wicomico County's theaters were concentrated in Salisbury, where Green and Brewington were showing movies by 1911. The 1947 thousand-seat Boulevard, the largest on the Eastern Shore, was nearly saved but had deteriorated so much that the effort failed. Willards had movies in 1909. The movie theaters of Worcester County were in Ocean City, Berlin, Snow Hill, and Pocomoke City. The Mar-Va Theater there has been saved and is being restored.

Grand Opera House, Cambridge, Md.

The Grand Opera House (9 Race Street, Cambridge) opened in October 1913. From the beginning, it presented movies and live stage shows. The first play given there was *Kindling* in November 1913. It was closed by 1948, when it was remodeled into a store.

CRISFIELD, MD.

The Lyric Theater (411 West Main Street, Crisfield) shared a block with the Majestic Theater (on Fifth Street) and the Opera House. It was open by 1912 and may have been the "handsome amusement building," designed by Jacob F. Gerwig, that was announced in 1909. (Photograph courtesy of the Library of Congress, Prints and Photographs Division, Wittemann Collection, LC-USZ62-57864.)

This photograph, taken around 1906, shows part of Dreamland at popular Tolchester Beach in Kent County. Like most of the amusement parks and larger beach resorts in the state, Tolchester had a small movie concession.

The Easton Academy of Music at Dover and Washington Streets opened in 1870. Movies were shown in the second-floor auditorium for a number of years. The building was converted into office space, and over the years, the auditorium disappeared behind new walls. During renovations in 2003, the auditorium was rediscovered. (Photograph courtesy of the Library of Congress, Prints and Photographs Division, Wittemann Collection, LC-USZ62-135156.)

The Centreville Opera House (177–178 Commerce Street, Centreville) opened in 1907. It was used for movies many times over the years until it was destroyed by fire in 1968. The opera house was a multipurpose auditorium with space for a billiard parlor and bowling alleys; it also housed the Good Will Fire Company. The auditorium, which seated about 600, was used for school graduations, spelling contests, and live theatricals, in addition to movies.

The auditorium or opera house (404 Main Street, Princess Anne) was open as early as 1911. It seated about 300 people and lasted until the 1950s, by which time Main Street had become Somerset Avenue.

THE CASINO THEATRE, OCEAN CITY, MD.

The early movie theaters in Ocean City were located along the boardwalk, as these two illustrations show. The Casino was operating as early as 1914.

The Pier, Ocean City, Md.

The Ocean City Pier probably dates from about the same time as the Casino. Many summer amusement parks in Maryland, including Electric Park, Riverview Park, and Luna Park in Baltimore, Bay Shore in Baltimore County, Tolchester and Betterton in Kent County, and Braddock Heights in Frederick County, had moving picture shows. (Photograph courtesy of William Hollifield.)

Betterton, located in Kent County at the mouth of the Sassafras River, along with Tolchester Beach, was a popular beach resort for Baltimoreans. The Rigbie Hotel was built there in 1902. Other hotels followed, and soon Betterton could host several thousand visitors. The Turner family had a large two-story pier with a dance pavilion where movies were shown. (Photograph courtesy of William Hollifield.)

NEW ARCADE THEATRE, AT NIGHT, SALISBURY, MD.

The Arcade Theater (Main Street, Salisbury) opened with an impressive show on December 24, 1914. The first presentation featured the George Evans "Honey Boy" Minstrels, who were described as a "company of sixty corkers with two cars of scenery, [a] street band and orchestra." Tickets cost from 50¢ to $2, ten times the usual prices. A devastating fire in January 1946 destroyed the Arcade.

The Mar-Va Theater (103 Market Street, Pocomoke City) opened in 1927. The interior was remodeled in 1937 in the art deco–style. After it closed in 1996, a group of local volunteers formed the Mar-Va Theater Performing Arts Center, Inc., and purchased the theater. Thanks to grants from the state and Worcester County, the Mar-Va is being restored.

The Churchill Theater was built in 1929 as a community hall. Motion picture equipment was installed, and movies were shown there beginning in late 1935. The building was remodeled with an art deco–style entrance after a fire in 1944. After it closed in the early 1980s, it was acquired by a nonprofit organization. It has been recycled as a successful performing arts venue.

The Federal Theater (115 North Main Street, Federalsburg) replaced the Federalsburg Town Hall as the town's major venue for entertainment. The 1867 town hall had been moved twice before; once around 1919 when the Masonic temple was built. The Masonic temple showed movies in a second-floor auditorium. The $60,000 Federal was erected in just 10 weeks on the site of the town hall in the fall of 1931. It was one of the many theaters designed by John J. Zink.

After closing in 1993 and being used as a store for a number of years, the Lyceum Theater (210 High Street, Chestertown), with its yellow brick facade, was restored and reopened as a performing arts center in 2002. It was designed by Baltimore architect A. Lowther Forrest and opened as the New Lyceum in 1928.

The Arcade Theater (102 Race Street, Cambridge) seated almost 900 people. It opened as the Cambridge Theater in September 1921 and lasted well into the 1950s. The Arcade was designed by Ernest J. Brannock for the Dorchester Amusement Company.

The town of Ridgely in Caroline County had movies as early as November 1911 when they were exhibited at Simon's Hall every Saturday night. There was a movie theater there by 1922. The theater pictured here is the Ridgely Theater around 1937. (Postcard photograph courtesy of Sonny Callahan.)

When it opened in June 1947, the art deco–style Boulevard Theater (317 East Main Street, Salisbury) was the largest movie theater on the Eastern Shore. It was designed for the Ulman Theater Corporation by Newell Howard and Raymond Todd. It seated 1,105 people and featured a nursery and party room on the balcony. The Boulevard closed in 2000. Heroic efforts to save it failed, and it was slated for demolition in 2007. (Photograph from the Otis R. Parker Collection, courtesy of the Edward H. Nabb Research Center for Delmarva History and Culture, Salisbury University, Salisbury, Maryland.)

Eight

FOSSIL THEATERS

Like bugs preserved in amber or dinosaur footprints embedded in stone, some movie theaters were preserved for years after their lives as theaters had ended. In a few cases, this was on purpose, but in most cases, it was a happy accident. Many of these fossils have disappeared under waves of urban renewal, but a few remain. On the following pages are pictures of some of these fossils.

Look closely to see bits of preserved movie theaters, perhaps just the outline of a facade, perhaps the trace of an entrance arch, perhaps a name implanted in the sidewalk or threshold as at the Linwood, Elk, and Roy Theaters, or perhaps not much has changed, as at the Eureka. Much of the Glen Theater in Glen Burnie is still there, including traces of the ticket booth. The entrance to the Elk Theater in Elkton was purposely left intact with the poster cases, terrazzo floor, and ticket booth, but the interior has been converted into office space. Much of the Bel-Air Theater remains, but it is scarcely recognizable. Parts of Baltimore's McHenry Theater, including the Light Street entrance and portions of the auditorium, are still there. The scars left by the balcony of Baltimore's Maryland Theater can still be seen on the walls of the Congress Hotel. Bits of an ancient sign for the Popular Theater in Baltimore have been found on one of the building's walls. The wonderful facade of the Colonial Theater in Hagerstown still graces South Potomac Street, even though it has not been a theater for many years. There are even remnants of a few of the state's drive-ins, including the 213 Drive-In near Church Hill and the General Pulaski Drive-In in White Marsh.

But too often the only trace of a theater is a vacant lot. There are no traces of some of the greatest theaters in the state. Baltimore's Stanley, Century, Ford's, Westport, Grand, and Lyceum have disappeared completely. The Hyattsville Theater, the Lyric in Crisfield, Ulman's Grand Opera House in Salisbury, the Strand and the Maryland in Cumberland, the Seco Theater in Rockville, and the Academy of Music in Hagerstown have all vanished, along with countless, smaller neighborhood theaters.

Only the scars of the balcony of the Maryland Theater (320 West Franklin Street, Baltimore) remain on the walls of the adjacent Congress Hotel. Soon after it closed in 1951, the Maryland was torn down, leaving only these traces. To see what the Maryland Theater looked like, see page 12.

The tiny New Windsor Theater (256 Main Street, New Windsor) was open as early as 1926 and as late as 1947. It probably closed in the 1950s. It was still standing as late as the mid-1970s when this photograph was taken, but it has now disappeared.

The Blue Bell (1713 Harford Avenue, Baltimore) operated between 1909 and 1925. It was built for about $5,000 and seated about 300 people. After being used as a church for a number of years, it was demolished in the 1980s.

Much of the facade of the attractive, little Preston Theater (1108 East Preston Street, Baltimore) remains to show what a nickelodeon looked like. Compare this with the photograph of the Preston on page 22.

Eugene McCurdy and William Kolb opened the Eureka Theater (400 South Fremont Avenue, Baltimore) in 1908. It became an African American theater in December 1951 and closed a year later. After many years as a church, it was demolished to make way for Martin Luther King Boulevard in 1973.

The remains of the Eureka's projection booth can be seen suspended from the back corner of the ceiling as the wreckers destroy the theater.

120

Sadly, the latest remodeling of this little nickelodeon has obliterated the name set in bricks at the top of the white, glazed-brick facade. This loss notwithstanding, the facade is still an attractive reminder of the Superba (906 Washington Boulevard, Baltimore), which showed movies from 1910 to 1935.

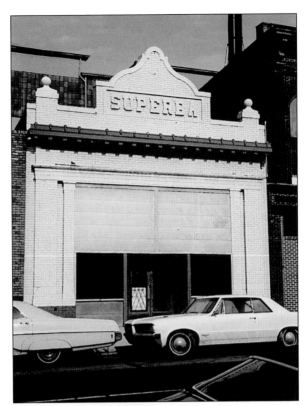

The Curtis Theater (4704 Curtis Avenue) operated in Curtis Bay for a few years in the 1920s. It closed around 1926, but the building lasted almost to the end of the 20th century. Little is known about its history. It may have been operated by a man named Shimanauskas.

This sidewalk sign was all that remained to show that a movie theater had been located in the 700 block of the Washington Boulevard, and the sign had disappeared by 2000. The theater opened as the Crown around 1908. It became the Roy in 1934 and closed as the Pic in 1950.

The tile sign provides the only evidence that the building at 902–904 South Linwood Avenue in Baltimore was ever the Linwood Theater. The Linwood was one of the first movie houses built by successful Baltimore exhibitor Charles E. Nolte. It opened in 1915 as an open-air theater and closed in 1952.

William Hollifield discovered and photographed this interesting trace of the Popular Theater (later the Astor) in West Baltimore. It can be found on the side wall of the old theater building at 611 Poplar Grove Street. See page 22 for a photograph of the Astor. (Photograph by and courtesy of William Hollifield.)

The Elk Theater (223 North Street, Elkton) opened in April 1949. It was one of the many theaters built after World War II by Sidney Lust. The Elk replaced the New Theater, which had been destroyed by fire two years earlier. When the Elk closed in February 1985, it was the last single-screen theater in Cecil County. Much of the exterior of the theater, including its name on the entrance floor, remains intact, but the interior has been remodeled into city offices.

The Edmondson Drive-In (6026 Baltimore National Pike, Catonsville) entertained carloads of patrons from May 1954 until 1991. It was such a success that its owners were able to build the adjoining Westview Theater (later a theater complex). A popular flea market was held there on Sundays. Since the drive-in closed, a Home Depot store and an adjoining parking lot have taken over the space.

SELECT BIBLIOGRAPHY

Allegany High School Social Studies Department. *Reflections of the Silver Screen. A History of Allegany County Movie Theatres.* Cumberland, MD: Allegany High School, 2000.

Allen, Robert C. and Douglas Gomery. *Film History: Theory and Practice.* New York: Alfred A. Knopf, 1985.

Durham, Weldon B. *Liberty Theatres of the United States Army, 1917-1919.* Jefferson, NC: McFarland and Company, Inc., 2006.

Gomery, Douglas. *The Hollywood Studio System.* New York: St. Martin's Press, 1986.

———. *Shared Pleasures.* Madison, WI: The University of Wisconsin Press, 1992.

Hall, Ben M. *The Best Remaining Seats: The Story of the Golden Age of the Movie Palace.* New York: Bramhall House, 1961.

Headley, Robert K. *EXIT: A History of Movies in Baltimore.* University Park, MD, 1974

———. *Motion Picture Exhibition in Washington, D.C.: An Illustrated History of Parlors, Palaces and Multiplexes in the Metropolitan Area, 1894-1997.* Jefferson, NC: McFarland and Company, Inc., 1999

———. "Early Movies in Annapolis 1901-1922," *Anne Arundel County History Notes,* Vol. XXXIV, No. 4 (July 2003), pp. 1-2, 6-8.

———. "Motion Picture Exhibition in Baltimore County," *History Trails of Baltimore County,* Vol. 36, Nos. 1-2 (Fall 2003), whole number.

———. *Motion Picture Exhibition in Baltimore: An Illustrated History and Directory of Theaters, 1895-2004.* Jefferson, NC: McFarland and Company, Inc., 2006

Hollifield, William. "The History of Motion Picture Exhibition in Towson," *History Trails of Baltimore County,* Vol. 38, Nos. 3-4, Vol. 39, Nos. 1-2 (Spring 2007), whole number.

Heathcote, Edwin. *Cinema Builders.* Chichester, England: Wiley-Academy, 2001

Kelbaugh, Jack. "The Star Anne Arundel's Only Black Movie Theater," *Anne Arundel County History Notes,* Vol. XXXI, No. 1 (October 1999), pp. 3-4, 9.

Melnick, Ross and Andreas Fuchs. *Cinema Treasures.* St. Paul, MN: MBI, 2004

Morrison, Craig. *Theaters.* New York and London: W. W. Norton and Company, 2006

Naylor, David. *American Picture Palaces: The Architecture of Fantasy.* New York: Van Nostrand Reinhold, 1981.

Waller, Gregory A., ed. *Moviegoing in America.* Oxford: Blackwell, 2002

White, Roger. "Circle Theatre," *Anne Arundel County History Notes,* Vol. XXVI, No. 1 (October 1994), pp. 7-8, 17.

———. "Capitol Theatre," *Anne Arundel County History Notes,* Vol. XXVI, No. 2 (January 1995), p. 9.

———. "Shows and Shoppers: Glen Burnie's Shopping Center Movie Theatres," *Anne Arundel County History Notes,* Vol. XXVII, No. 3 (April 1996), pp. 5, 11-12.

———. "Movie Theatres in Parole," *Anne Arundel County History Notes,* Vol. XXXVI, No. 1 (October 2004), pp. 3-4, 9.

INDEX

ACROSS AMERICA, PEOPLE ARE DISCOVERING SOMETHING WONDERFUL. *THEIR HERITAGE.*

Arcadia Publishing is the leading local history publisher in the United States. With more than 4,000 titles in print and hundreds of new titles released every year, Arcadia has extensive specialized experience chronicling the history of communities and celebrating America's hidden stories, bringing to life the people, places, and events from the past. To discover the history of other communities across the nation, please visit:

www.arcadiapublishing.com

Customized search tools allow you to find regional history books about the town where you grew up, the cities where your friends and family live, the town where your parents met, or even that retirement spot you've been dreaming about.